The
Kent State Shootings

by Natalie M. Rosinsky

Content Adviser: Alan Canfora,
Director, Kent May 4 Center,
Kent, Ohio

Reading Adviser: Alexa L. Sandmann, Ed.D.,
Professor of Literacy, College and Graduate School of Education,
Kent State University

Compass Point Books ✦ Minneapolis, Minnesota

Compass Point Books
151 Good Counsel Drive
P.O. Box 669
Mankato, MN 56002-0669

 This book was manufactured with paper containing
at least 10 percent post-consumer waste.

On the cover: Ohio National Guardsmen armed with rifles and bayonets approached students
on the Kent State University campus.

Photographs ©: Kent State University Libraries, Special Collections and Archives, cover, 8, 9, 16,
18, 19, 20, 27, 28, 36; Prints Old & Rare, back cover (far left); Library of Congress, back cover, 23;
John Filo/Getty Images, 4; Howard Ruffner/Time & Life Pictures/Getty Images, 6; Blank Archives/
Getty Images, 10; Bettman/Corbis, 11, 22, 33; Bernard Gotfryd/Getty Images, 13; Corbis, 14; Wally
McNamee/Corbis, 29; AP Images/Jack Thornell, 30; 1970 John Paul Filo, all rights reserved, 35; AP
Images, 39; AP Images/*The Plain Dealer*/John Kuntz, 40.

Managing Editor: Catherine Neitge
Art Director/Page Production: LuAnn Ascheman-Adams
Photo Researcher: Robert McConnell
Cartographer: XNR Productions, Inc.
Library Consultant: Kathleen Baxter

Creative Director: Keith Griffin
Editorial Director: Nick Healy

Library of Congress Cataloging-in-Publication Data
Rosinsky, Natalie M. (Natalie Myra)
  The Kent State shootings / by Natalie M. Rosinsky.
     p. cm.
  Includes index.
ISBN 978-0-7565-3845-3 (library binding)
1. Kent State Shootings, Kent, Ohio, 1970—Juvenile literature. 2. Kent State University—
Students—Political activity—History—20th century—Juvenile literature. I. Title.
  LD4191.O72R67 2009
  378.771'37—dc22   2008009481

Visit Compass Point Books on the Internet at *www.compasspointbooks.com*
or e-mail your request to *custserv@compasspointbooks.com*

TABLE OF CONTENTS

"The War Had Come Into Our Town"

Fourteen-year-old Mary Ann Vecchio screamed "Oh, my God!" She knelt next to the body of Jeffrey Miller, who had just been shot in the head. Mary's earlier excitement at

A photo of Mary Ann Vecchio screaming over the body of Jeffrey Miller won a Pulitzer Prize and became a symbol of the antiwar movement.

4

being part of a college student protest against the Vietnam War had become a nightmare.

Horror and shock spread as people realized how much violence had just occurred on the campus of Kent State University in Ohio. It seemed impossible. May 4, 1970, was a beautiful spring day. The sky was a brilliant blue, and pleasant breezes rustled the blooming dogwood trees. Yet in merely 13 seconds on that sunny Monday afternoon, rifles fired by 28 Ohio National Guardsmen killed four college students and injured nine others. The guardsmen later claimed they fired because they feared their own lives were in danger. Investigations that followed cast doubt on their claim.

Miller, age 20, had been a sophomore majoring in psychology. Raised on Long Island, New York, he had been active in the protest. Allison Krause, a 19-year-old honors student from Pittsburgh, Pennsylvania, also opposed the war. As she felt a bullet strike her back, Allison murmured to her boyfriend, "Barry, I'm hit." By the time the ambulance carrying her reached the hospital, she was dead.

National Guard soldiers wore gas masks as they marched toward Kent State students.

William Schroeder was a 19-year-old sophomore majoring in psychology. A native of Lorain, Ohio, he was serving in the Army Reserve Officers' Training Corps (ROTC) to help pay his way through college. Schroeder was merely observing the demonstration from the sidelines when he was shot in the back. The bullet pierced his body and killed him.

ABOUT THE WAR

The Vietnam War was fought from 1959 to 1975. South Vietnam battled the communist Viet Cong of the South and the communists of North Vietnam. (Communists believe in an economic system in which goods and property are owned by the government and shared in common. Communist rulers limit personal freedoms to achieve their goals.)

The Viet Cong and the North Vietnamese wanted to unite the two countries into one communist nation. They were backed by the Soviet Union and China. The United States supported the South Vietnamese with money and troops. The first American combat troops arrived in 1965. By early 1968, there were more than 500,000 U.S. troops fighting in Vietnam.

The fighting grew costly in lives and money. Protests against the war increased. In 1973, a cease-fire agreement was reached, and U.S. troops were withdrawn. Fighting continued, however, until 1975, when the North took control of a united Vietnam.

The war killed more than 58,000 Americans and between 2 million and 4 million Vietnamese. More than 300,000 Americans were wounded during the war, the longest in U.S. history. The effects of the long, bloody war are still felt today.

Sandra Scheuer

Twenty-year-old Sandra Scheuer, from Youngstown, Ohio, was another spectator. A sophomore majoring in speech and hearing therapy, she was hurrying across campus to her next class. A bullet tore through her throat and killed her.

The injured students included 20-year-old Dean Kahler, who later recalled his back "felt as if it had been touched by a live wire" when a bullet pierced it. Kahler was permanently paralyzed and has used a wheelchair since that day. Eighteen-year-old Joseph Lewis nearly died from the bullets that tore through his side. He required several surgeries.

The other students wounded that day were Alan Canfora, John Cleary, Thomas Grace, Donald Scott

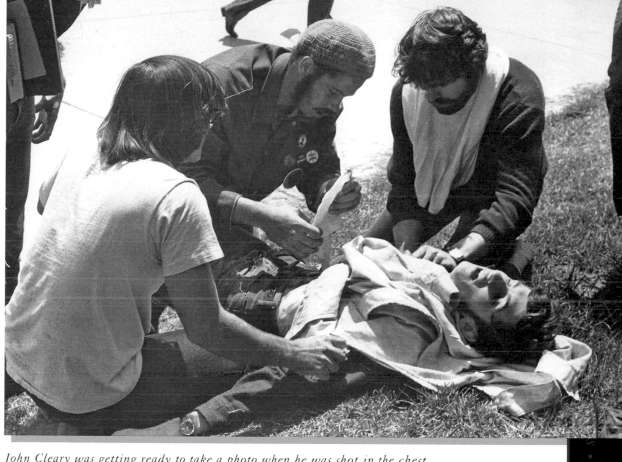

John Cleary was getting ready to take a photo when he was shot in the chest.

MacKenzie, James Russell, Robert Stamps, and Douglas
Wrentmore. They ranged in age from 19 to 21 years old.
Like the four slain students, some of these young men were
involved in the protest, while others were just bystanders or
on their way to class.

9

*Many students wore antiwar buttons
during the Vietnam War.*

As news of the Kent State shootings reached officials in the city of Kent and surrounding communities, public schools shut down and students were sent home. Mary Ohles Black was an 11-year-old fifth-grader in Kent. She recalled feeling as though "the [Vietnam] war had come into our town."

Mary was right in several ways. Protests against the Vietnam War had led to a troubled weekend around the country that sparked the Kent State shootings. Like the Vietnam War itself, these shootings remain a source of bitter arguments and strong emotions.

"FLOWERS ARE BETTER THAN BULLETS"

Protests against the Vietnam War took different forms. Some of the first campus protests in 1965 were called teach-ins. They were gatherings at which students, teachers, and guest speakers discussed the war for hours in front of large audiences. Sometimes college students would burn their draft cards in demonstrations against the war.

Students took their protests off campus, too. In April 1965, a nationwide student group called

Thousands of students protested near the White House in April 1965.

11

Students for a Democratic Society (SDS) organized the first large antiwar march in Washington, D.C. At least 25,000 people traveled to the nation's capital. As the United States sent more combat troops to Vietnam, antiwar demonstrations increased in size and frequency. Students and other pacifists took part in these demonstrations. They carried signs and wore buttons urging people to "Resist." They asked, "What would happen if they gave a war and nobody came?"

By 1968, students at more than 1,500 colleges and universities around the United States were protesting the war. For the most part, the protests were peaceful, but sometimes they unexpectedly turned violent. A few student protest groups—such as the Weathermen, organized in 1969—believed violence was an effective way to draw attention to their cause. They deliberately damaged property or started fights during demonstrations.

News of military activities in Vietnam, such as the lengthy Tet Offensive and the My Lai massacre of Vietnamese civilians by U.S. troops, sparked more antiwar

A protester wearing peace symbols and military medals marched in New York City in 1969.

demonstrations in 1968 and 1969. Then, in 1969, President Richard M. Nixon began withdrawing some U.S. troops from Vietnam. This new U.S. policy was called Vietnamization, and it involved leaving trained South Vietnamese forces to fight more battles.

However, on April 30, 1970, Nixon shocked the nation with a televised speech announcing a U.S. military

President Richard Nixon explained his Cambodian policy to a stunned nation in 1970.

invasion of Cambodia, a country located next to Vietnam. He also revealed that for months U.S. troops had been secretly fighting North Vietnamese forces in Cambodia. This news seemed to betray the Vietnamization policy by spreading the war to another country. Nixon had been elected in 1968 on a campaign promise to end the war in Vietnam and bring "peace with honor."

The day after the president's speech, outraged students began demonstrating on campuses across the nation. At Kent State University on Friday, May 1, about 500 protesters buried a copy of the U.S. Constitution. They said Nixon had similarly "murdered" American ideals by sending troops into Cambodia. That night, crowds of students and other protesters broke windows and damaged property in downtown Kent. Worried that further violence would occur in the community of 50,000 people, Mayor Leroy Satrom declared a "state of emergency." He ordered city police wearing riot gear to use tear gas to break up the crowds. The mayor also phoned Governor James Rhodes for help.

On Saturday, May 2, rumors spread throughout Kent. Officials feared that violent protesters were coming to their community. By 8 o'clock that night, more than 600 protesters surrounded the wooden ROTC building on campus. Someone set it on fire and then cut the fire hoses, which prevented firefighters from putting out the blaze. Governor Rhodes ordered the National Guard to go to Kent. Using tear gas and prodding people with bayonets, they forced protesters to return to student dormitories or leave the campus.

On Sunday, May 3, students awoke to find 800 soldiers on the Kent State campus. They had stayed overnight in Army tents. Four hundred more guardsmen were stationed in the city. That morning in Kent, Rhodes told reporters that student protesters who commit violent acts are "the worst type of people that we harbor in America." The leader of Ohio's National Guard, General Sylvester Del Corso, promised reporters that the Guard would maintain order "like the Ohio law says." He added that they would "use any force that is necessary even to the point of shooting."

National Guardsmen patrolled near the burned ROTC building.

During the day, the Kent State campus remained
calm. Allison Krause even chatted with some National
Guardsmen there. As her boyfriend, Barry Levine, later

The guardsmen's rifles held live ammunition and bayonets.

remembered, Krause asked one, "What's the matter with peace? Flowers are better than bullets." That night, though, students began to protest the presence of the guardsmen on campus. Several hundred students chanted, staged a sit-in, and refused to return to their dormitories. National Guardsmen broke up these demonstrations with tear gas and bayonets, stabbing several students. Fifty-one people were arrested. Noisy military helicopters flew overhead, shining spotlights on the dark campus.

William Schroeder

William Schroeder had spent the weekend off campus on a family visit. When he returned to his dormitory that Sunday night, he was disturbed by the helicopters' lights and noise. Before falling asleep, he told his roommate, Lou Cusella, "I'm scared, Louie." Those were the last words Cusella ever heard Schroeder say.

TEAR GAS, CHAOS, AND TRAGEDY

On Monday, May 4, officials at Kent State University planned to hold classes as normal. They had already passed out leaflets forbidding student demonstrations that day.

Ohio Guardsmen marched toward the students on May 4.

Yet things were not normal. City and state officials had not lifted the weekend's state of emergency. National Guardsmen dressed in combat gear still remained on campus. A previously scheduled rally on the large grassy area called the Commons was still planned for noon. The local National Guard leader, General Robert Canterbury, was determined to prevent the demonstration.

At noon, about 2,000 students were walking through or standing on the Commons. Classes had ended at 11:50 A.M., and about half of those students were heading to their next class, going to lunch, or walking back to their dormitories. Some were taking a shortcut through a nearby parking lot. About 500 or so people were watching the roughly 500 students gathered for the rally.

The protesters did not obey a shouted order to leave. Some may not have heard the order. They continued to chant and yell at the guardsmen. Some students threw rocks at them. Shortly after noon, the National Guard fired canisters of tear gas into the crowd. The soldiers moved forward, using

Students ran from the tear gas and bullets fired by the guardsmen.

the bayonets on their rifles to force demonstrators up the hill to Taylor Hall. More tear gas, shouts, and rocks were exchanged as guardsmen pushed the students toward an athletic field. It was 12:24 P.M. when Douglas Wrentmore remembered hearing "a volley of shots."

22

Ohio National Guardsmen began firing at 12:24 P.M.

Wrentmore, a sophomore, was shot in the leg. He had been in the parking lot watching the demonstration. Interviewed the next day by a reporter, he said, "Girls started screaming. I saw people fall, and I started running and then I fell. I didn't feel anything. One minute I could run and then I could not. Then I saw blood coming from my leg." He added, "I just don't understand why the troops fired into the crowd."

The National Guardsmen later defended their actions. Guardsman Larry Schaefer shot a student who was making a rude gesture with one hand but had his other arm behind his back. Schaefer said, "I felt I was in immediate danger, not knowing whether he had a weapon or a rock [hidden]." Another guardsmen said, "We were surrounded and outnumbered 10 to one. You should have seen those animals. They were trying to take away our rifles." General Canterbury also insisted that "the situation was dangerous." He said, "I felt I could be killed." The general added that many students were throwing baseball-sized rocks and con-crete slabs at guardsmen.

Other reports contradicted the general's observation. They agreed with Wrentmore, who saw only about a dozen students throwing sticks and rocks at the guardsmen. According to Wrentmore, these rocks were "just pebbles,

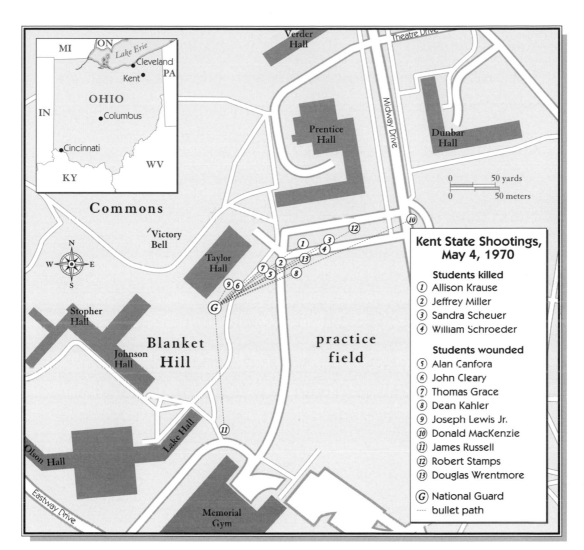

Thirteen Kent State University students were in the guardsmen's line of fire.

with a few maybe the size of a golf ball." The slain and

wounded students were also too far away from the shooters

to have hit them with heavy rocks. Investigators discovered

that the closest victim—Joseph Lewis—was 20 yards (18.2 meters) away. Most victims were between 70 yards and 200 yards (63.7 m and 182.8 m) away. (A football field, including end zones, for example, is 120 yards long.) Investigators also concluded that the guardsmen were not surrounded and could have continued going forward.

After the volley of 67 shots was over, Alan Canfora, a student who was injured, recalled "kind of an eerie calm, just for a second." He said, "We waited to hear if there were any more bullets that were going to be fired, and there were none. And then, all you could hear in the air after that was screaming, crying, people shouting for ambulances."

CAMPUSES UNITE IN PROTEST

At first, newscasts did not name the slain and injured students. When Jeffrey Miller's mother tried to reach him by phone, she was told, "He's dead." When Allison Krause's mother asked about her injured daughter, a hospital official, seemingly without sympathy, replied, "Oh, she was DOA (dead on arrival)." In the following months, the four grieving families dealt with remarks and letters from some people who believed that student protesters deserved to be shot.

Most Americans, however, were shocked by the

Allison Krause

27

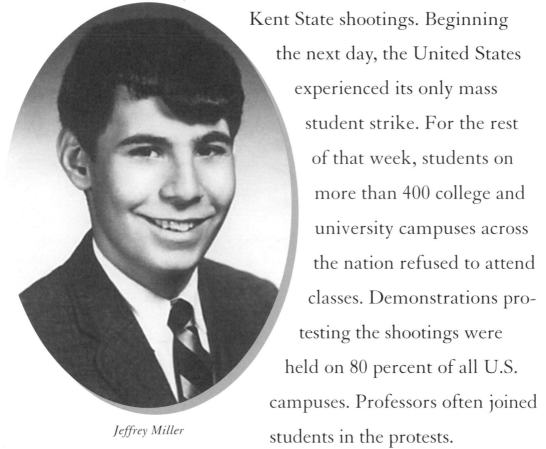

Jeffrey Miller

Kent State shootings. Beginning the next day, the United States experienced its only mass student strike. For the rest of that week, students on more than 400 college and university campuses across the nation refused to attend classes. Demonstrations protesting the shootings were held on 80 percent of all U.S. campuses. Professors often joined students in the protests.

On May 9, more than 100,000 people surrounded the White House in Washington, D.C., in a demonstration against both the Kent State shootings and the deployment of U.S. troops in Cambodia. President Nixon later wrote that the days following the shootings were "among the darkest" of his presidency. Soon after these events, he announced that

The shootings at Kent State escalated the protests against the Vietnam War.

U.S. troops would leave Cambodia within two months.

Another similar tragedy occurred just days after the Kent State shootings. On May 14 and 15, city police fired into a crowd of student protesters at Jackson State College (now University) in Jackson, Mississippi. They killed a college student, Philip Lafayette Gibbs, who was shot four times, and a high school student, James Earl Green. The 17-year-old Green was walking home from work when he

Police riddled Jackson State dorm windows with bullets during an altercation with protesters.

was struck. Gunfire injured 12 other Jackson State students, including one who was sitting inside a dormitory lobby.

Three weeks after the Kent State shootings, the musical group Crosby, Stills, Nash, and Young wrote and recorded a song about the event titled "Ohio." It included the lines: "Tin soldiers and Nixon's coming/We're finally on our own/This summer I hear the drumming/Four dead in Ohio." Radios broadcast the song throughout the next months, as the President's Commission on Campus Unrest investigated the events of May 4. In September, its members concluded that the soldiers' firing of weapons was "unnecessary, unwarranted, and inexcusable." They declared that this must be "the last time that loaded rifles are issued as a matter of course to guardsmen confronting student demonstrators." The commission's report also stated, however, that "violent and criminal" actions by students contributed to the tragedy.

The report offered little comfort or satisfaction to the families of the slain and injured students. Grief-stricken Sarah Scheuer continued to blame herself unreasonably for a red shirt she had just given her daughter. Sandra Scheuer wore this gift on May 4. According to a lawyer who represented the families, Mrs. Scheuer was convinced that "someone had aimed at Sandy's red shirt. If Sandy hadn't been wearing the red shirt ... Sandy would still be with them."

"BETTER WAYS MUST BE FOUND"

Overlapping investigations continued about whom to blame, charge, and punish for the Kent State shootings. University President Robert White formed a school commission on May 11 to gather information. White spoke to this commission, to President Nixon's Commission on Campus Unrest, and to FBI agents conducting a separate Justice Department investigation. In their statements, White and General Canterbury disagreed about each other's responsibilities on May 4. In 1971, White resigned from his job.

None of these or later investigations led to criminal charges against guardsmen who had shot the students. Although eight guardsmen were indicted on federal civil rights charges and arrested in 1974 following a grand jury investigation, the charges were later dismissed.

In October 1970, the state of Ohio charged 25 protesters with destroying property during the weekend of May 1–4. Known as the Kent 25, these students bitterly joked that

None of the Ohio National Guardsmen were punished for their role in the shootings.

"the ones they [government officials] missed with bullets, they got with indictments." Two of the men pleaded guilty. Another man was convicted of interfering with a firefighter and sentenced to six months in jail. There was not enough evidence to convict the other 22 protesters.

During these and other investigations, several rumors spread. Some people claimed that a sniper's gunshot had

33

startled the guardsmen into shooting at students. But an FBI investigation concluded that no one but the guardsmen fired guns. Other people wondered if the guardsmen had planned among themselves to shoot the students. They said that photos showing the guardsmen huddled together were evidence of such a conspiracy. They believed that the guardsmen's firing at the same time also suggested a plot.

Other people on campus that day claimed to have heard a soldier give an order to fire on the students. This would also explain the guardsmen's shooting together. A recently enhanced tape recording from May 4, 1970, indicates to some listeners that an order to fire was issued. They say they can hear the words "Right here. Get set. Point. Fire." But others are skeptical. The tape and the rumors are still being examined nearly 40 years after the shootings.

The families of the slain and wounded students sued the state of Ohio, Governor Rhodes, and the National Guard. They wanted an apology for the shootings and enough money to help Dean Kahler, who was paralyzed.

Alan Canfora, who waved his homemade flag before guardsmen regrouped and started shooting, today heads the nonprofit Kent May 4 Center, an educational charity.

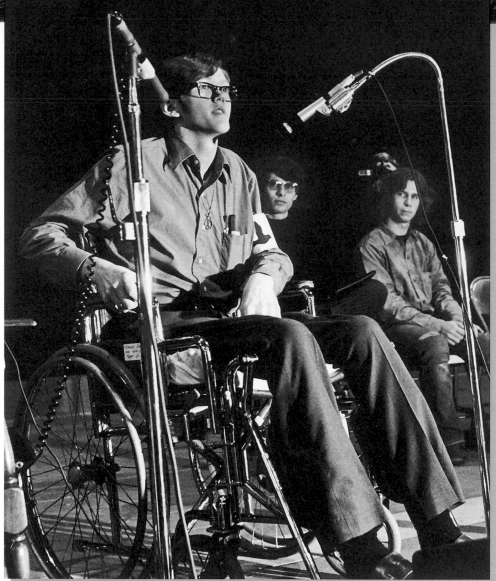

Dean Kahler has been paralyzed from the chest down since he was shot on May 4, 1970.

Complicated laws dragged out these legal battles until 1979.
The victims and their families then accepted an out-of-court
settlement of $675,000. Kahler received $350,000 of this

amount. For the deaths of their loved ones, each family received only $15,000.

The settlement also included a statement signed by Rhodes, General Del Corso, and 26 National Guardsmen. It was not the full apology the surviving victims and all of their families wanted. Instead, it began by noting that both forbidding the protest and stationing guardsmen on campus were "lawful" acts. The statement then read, "We devoutly wish that a means had been found to avoid the May events. ... We deeply regret these events and are profoundly saddened by the deaths of four students and wounding of nine others. ... Better ways must be found to deal with such confrontations."

The surviving victims and their families responded with their own statement. They wrote that "For Allison, Sandra, Jeffrey, and William/For Peace and Justice" they hoped such "better ways" would become a new federal law.

MEMORIALS CONTINUE

Questions raised by the Kent State shootings continue to challenge people's minds and hearts. Every May 3 since 1971, a nightlong candlelight vigil has taken place on the campus where the four students were slain. A noon memorial service follows every May 4, the anniversary of the shootings and deaths. In 1999, markers with the names of the victims were installed to mark the site.

Not all of the ceremonies have been calm. In 1977, when Kent State planned to build a gym annex right next to the memorial site, more than 1,500 people protested. They felt that altering the site would show disrespect for the victims and historical events. Nearly 400 people were arrested, including the parents of Sandra Scheuer. Her father, Martin Scheuer, had joined the protest, saying, "I will be there under the bulldozers" if construction begins. Some students protested by living for weeks in a "tent city" on campus. Despite the demonstrations, Kent State University went ahead and built

An Ohio State Historical Marker was dedicated in May 2007, 37 years after the shootings.

the gym. Officials said they needed to honor their contracts with the builders.

The tent city controversy was a reminder of the widespread influence of the Kent State shootings. As the wounded

Thomas Grace once stated, "I enrolled in Kent State to study American history and, through no intention of my own, became a part of it." New federal and state guidelines for the use of force on campus did result from investigations into the shootings. Moreover, many historians believe that

Homemade tombstones representing soldiers killed in Iraq were erected during an annual May 4 memorial service at Kent State University.

public outrage over the events that day led President Nixon to withdraw troops from Cambodia. This hastened the end of the Vietnam War.

Twenty years after the shootings, a memorial over-looking the campus Commons was dedicated. Engraved on the granite floor of the plaza are the words, "Inquire, Learn, Reflect." The memorial is surrounded by 58,175 daffodils—the number of Americans killed in Vietnam. As visitors view this site, they are drawn to reflect not only on the violence suffered on May 4, 1970, but on the losses from the Vietnam War and other conflicts. Visitors are reminded that asking and learning about government decisions are important, valuable acts—the heart of a democracy.

GLOSSARY

bayonets—blades attached to the ends of rifles that are used as weapons in close combat

conspiracy—secret agreement between two or more people to commit a harmful or illegal act

controversy—matter of fact or opinion over which people strongly disagree

draft—system that chooses people who are compelled by law to serve in the military

draft card—piece of paper issued by the U.S. Selective Service System to show that a young man has registered for the draft

indictments—formal charges of committing a crime

pacifists—people who are opposed to war as a way of settling disagreements

strike—to stop work as a way of protest

vigil—staying awake for a particular purpose during normal sleeping hours

volley—rapid firing of guns or other weapons at the same time

DID YOU KNOW?

- In 1981, the NBC television network aired a docudrama about the shootings, titled *Kent State*. The television documentary *Kent State: The Day the War Came Home*, directed by Chris Triffo, won a 2001 Emmy Award. In 2008, a National Geographic Channel documentary *Death at Kent State* re-examined the shootings.

- The May 4th Task Force was founded on the Kent State campus in 1975 to heighten awareness of the tragedy. The group presents plays, films, and slide shows about the shooting and its aftermath.

- A bullet fired on May 4, 1970, at Kent State pierced a metal statue by sculptor Don Drumm. The bullet hole remains, and the statue is part of yearly memorial services. Drumm created a new monument, titled *Bridge Over Troubled Water,* and dedicated it to the victims of the shootings. It is displayed on the campus of Bowling Green State University in Ohio. George Segal created a sculpture, *Abraham and Isaac*, as a memorial to the students slain at Kent State. His work is displayed on the campus of Princeton University.

IMPORTANT DATES

Timeline

1970	April 30, President Richard Nixon announces the U.S. invasion of Cambodia; May 1, protests against troops in Cambodia begin at Kent State University and other college campuses; May 2, National Guard arrives on the Kent State campus; May 4, guardsmen shoot students at Kent State; May 5–8, college students strike nationwide to protest the shootings; May 9, demonstrators in Washington, D.C., protest the Kent State shootings and the presence of U.S. troops in Cambodia; May 14–15, police shoot students on the Jackson State College campus; in September, President's Commission on Campus Unrest issues its report about the Kent State shootings.
1973	In January, cease-fire is declared, ending the Vietnam War.
1977	In May, protests against a new gym annex near the site of the Kent State shootings lead students to build a tent city on campus.
1979	In January, a lawsuit by families of slain and wounded students is settled.

IMPORTANT PEOPLE

ALLISON KRAUSE (April 23, 1951–May 4, 1970)

Interested in art, philosophy, and literature, she had made plans with her boyfriend to transfer to another university in the fall of 1970; shortly after her death, famous Russian poet Yevgeny Yevtushenko wrote a poem dedicated to her, titled Flowers and Bullets

JEFFREY MILLER (March 28, 1950–May 4, 1970)

A recent transfer student from Michigan State University, he had been interested in the antiwar movement as a high school student; the Pulitzer Prize–winning photo of a girl in anguish over his lifeless body became a symbol of the antiwar movement

SANDRA LEE SCHEUER (August 11, 1949–May 4, 1970)

An honors student who loved animals, she was a speech and hearing therapy major and a member of Alpha Xi Delta sorority; she was walking beside one of the students she coached when she was shot; sorority members participate in the May 4 memorial service each year

WILLIAM KNOX SCHROEDER (July 20, 1950–May 4, 1970)

A psychology student and ROTC member, he had recently transferred to Kent State from the Colorado School of Mines; he loved the outdoors and sports; he was observing the demonstration when he was shot in the back and killed

WANT TO KNOW MORE?

More Books to Read

Caputo, Philip. *10,000 Days of Thunder: A History of the Vietnam War.*
New York: Atheneum Books for Young Readers, 2005.

Caputo, Philip. *13 Seconds: A Look Back at the Kent State Shootings.*
New York: Chamberlain Bros., 2005.

Dunn, John M. *The Vietnam War: A History of U.S. Involvement.*
San Diego: Lucent Books, 2001.

McCormick, Anita Louise. *The Vietnam Antiwar Movement in American
History.* Berkeley Heights, N.J.: Enslow Publishers, 2001.

Meltzer, Milton. *Ain't Gonna Study War No More: The Story of America's
Peace Seekers.* New York: Random House, 2002.

Zeinert, Karen. *The Valiant Women of the Vietnam War.* Brookfield, Conn.:
Millbrook Press, 2000.

On the Web

For more information on this topic, use FactHound.

1. Go to *www.facthound.com*

2. Type in this book ID: 0756538459

3. Click on the *Fetch It* button.

FactHound will find the best Web sites for you.

On the Road

May 4 Memorial
Kent State University
Kent, Ohio
330/672-3000
Outdoor monument designed by
architect Bruno Ast in honor of
the students shot and killed on
May 4, 1970; site of a yearly vigil
and memorial service

Abraham and Isaac
Princeton University Sculpture Garden
Princeton University
Princeton, New Jersey
609/258-3000
Statue created by sculptor George
Segal in memory of the students slain
and injured at Kent State University

Look for more We the People books about this era:

The 19th Amendment
The Berlin Airlift
The Civil Rights Act of 1964
The Draft Lottery
The Dust Bowl
Ellis Island
The Fall of Saigon
GI Joe in World War II
The Great Depression
The Holocaust Museum
The Korean War
The My Lai Massacre
Navajo Code Talkers

The Negro Leagues
Pearl Harbor
The Persian Gulf War
The San Francisco Earthquake of 1906
Selma's Bloody Sunday
September 11
The Sinking of the USS Indianapolis
The Statue of Liberty
The Tet Offensive
The Titanic
The Tuskegee Airmen
Vietnam Veterans Memorial
Vietnam War POWs

A complete list of We the People titles is available on our Web site:
www.compasspointbooks.com

INDEX

About the Author

Natalie M. Rosinsky is the award-winning author of more than 90 publications. She writes about history, social studies, economics, popular culture, and science. She has written several books about the Vietnam War era. Natalie earned graduate degrees from the University of Wisconsin-Madison and has been a high school teacher and college professor as well as a corporate trainer. She lives and writes in Mankato, Minnesota.